W9-ACM-234

Understanding Genetics™

The Human Genome

Bridget Heos

New York

To my husband, Justin

Published in 2011 by The Rosen Publishing Group, Inc.
29 East 21st Street, New York, NY 10010

Library of Congress Cataloging-in-Publication Data

Heos, Bridget.
The human genome / Bridget Heos.—1st ed.
    p. cm.—(Understanding genetics)
Includes bibliographical references and index.
ISBN 978-1-4358-9533-1 (library binding)
1. Human genome—Juvenile literature. 2. Genetics—Juvenile literature. I. Title.
QH437.5.H46 2011
611'.0181663—dc22

                                                            2009047915

Manufactured in the United States of America

CPSIA Compliance Information: Batch #S10YA: For further information, contact Rosen Publishing, New York, New York, at 1-800-237-9932.

On the cover: It took scientists almost a decade and a half to map the human genome.

Contents

Introduction

Imagine an enormous book . . . one that is three billion letters long! The title is *The Human Genome Cookbook.* It's about the human genome—the complete collection of human genes. Genes are the instructions for making proteins, which build the body and keep it running. If a gene were a recipe, the protein would be the actual food that the recipe makes. Each person has his or her own unique genome, but everybody's is similar.

The genome is like a cookbook because it's made up of chemical "letters," called nucleotide bases, which combine in threes. Together, three letters make a "word." Several words together make a gene, which is the recipe for making a protein.

Inside this so-called genome cookbook, there would be twenty-three chapters, one for each pair of chromosomes, including the chromosomes that determine whether a person is a girl, XX, or a boy, XY. Chromosomes are molecules made of the chemical DNA. DNA is comprised of thousands of recipes—the genes. Genes, in turn, are made from nucleotide bases. Three paired bases are the recipe for one amino acid. Amino acids come together in numerous combinations to make the proteins, which make all the structures of the body. Within each chromosome are thousands of recipes—the genes.

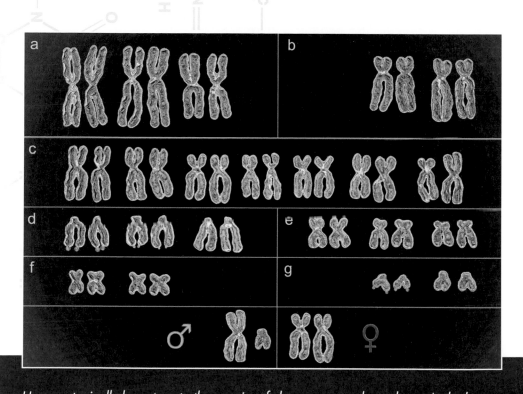

Humans typically have twenty-three pairs of chromosomes, shown here. At the bottom left is the XY chromosome pair, which boys have. Below, right, is the XX chromosome pair, which girls have.

If people read "cookbooks" about their own genomes, they would probably be most interested in the recipes that affect personality traits, such as shyness or risk-taking, or physical traits, such as height or hair color. If a disease ran in their family, they would want to know what gene mutation, or variation from the norm, caused it.

However, most recipes, or genes, are for basic life processes like making cells, tissues, and organs.

In this cookbook, for every one important paragraph, there are forty-nine paragraphs that have nothing to do with the recipe. These are what scientists used to call junk DNA. Junk DNA does not give instructions for making proteins. Scientists now think it has other important jobs, such as switching genes on and off. When a gene is on, it means it will be read to make the proteins that it codes for. When a gene is off, these proteins will not be made.

There's something else unusual about this cookbook. The recipes are disorganized. Chapter one does not focus on appearance, for instance, while chapter two deals with health, and chapter three, personality. Instead, the recipes are scattered haphazardly among the chromosomes. Hundreds of genes may impact a person's personality, for instance, and they are found on different chromosomes.

Mapping the human genome, a nearly decade-and-a-half-long project that was recently completed, was the greatest scientific accomplishment of the century. The genome shows us how we evolved. It teaches us how closely related humans are to each other—and to other plants and animals. The information it contains may provide cures that once seemed far away. It is the recipe for all life. Here is the story of the human genome.

CHAPTER one

The Basics of the Human Genome

W here is the human genome? Let's zoom in. The human body has between fifty and one hundred trillion (100,000,000,000,000) cells total, and around two hundred cell types. Different cells have different jobs. When a hair falls out, look at the follicle—or root—on the end that was attached to the head. That root contains about a million cells. In each cell there is a nucleus. Each nucleus contains two sets of the human genome (one from the mother, and one from the father.) There are exceptions: Egg or sperm cells have one set each. Red blood cells have none.

Inside the cell nucleus, the genome is scattered among the twenty-three chromosome pairs. Each pair consists of one chromosome from the mom and one from the dad. The chromosomes are made of a chemical called deoxyribonucleic acid, or DNA for short. DNA is shaped like a long twisted rope ladder, also known as a double helix. The "ladder" then wraps around proteins to condense them into smaller units, making a fiber called chromatin, which makes up chromosomes. On each "ladder rung" are two letters—either A and T, or G and C. In DNA, A is always paired with T and G with C.

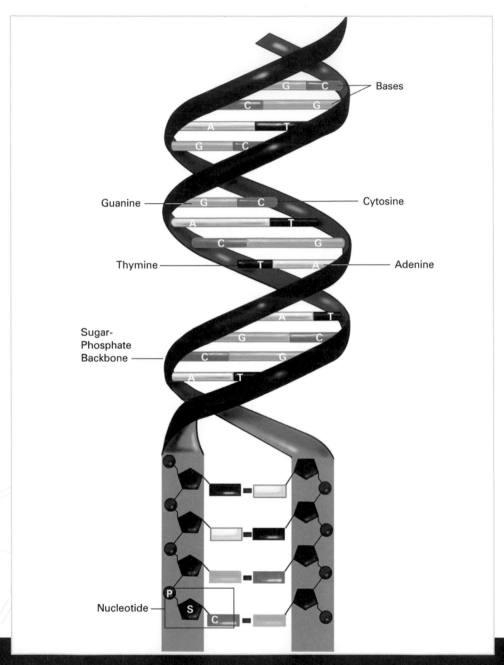

DNA is made up of two long, thin, twisted chains. Each chain consists of a sugar-phosphate backbone and a base. The bases can be adenine (A), thymine (T), cytosine (C), or guanine (G).

These letters stand for the chemical compounds adenine, thymine, guanine, and cytosine.

Reading the letters up and down along the ladder, they make three-letter words. The three-letter words are instructions for building amino acids. Amino acids work together to build proteins. Proteins are the building blocks of the body. They are responsible for both its structure (bones, muscles, etc.) and its functions (pumping blood, digesting food, etc.).

Several words together make up a gene. Some of these three-letter words are instructions for making amino acids. These are called exons. Others are not. Those are called introns. These non-coding words make up about 98 percent of the genome.

Introns used to be called junk DNA. Scientists now know that introns help regulate genes. Some of this DNA replicates itself and moves around in the genome. These sequences are called transposons. If they land in the wrong place, they can have devastating effects. For instance, if they appear in the middle of blood-clotting genes, they can cause hemophilia, a condition in which the blood cannot clot and a person cannot stop bleeding if injured. However, if transposons land in the right place, they can switch on genes that code for a helpful new function or structure, ultimately leading to the evolution of a species.

The genome contains three billion base pairs, making it as long as 2,400 bibles. And to think, a complete copy of an individual's genome exists in each of his or her fifty to one-hundred trillion cells! In each cell, only the genes needed for that specific cell's function are switched on; the others are switched off. For instance, in each cell in a hair follicle, the genes for making keratin, a hair protein, are turned on. The genes for, say, smelling are turned off.

From DNA to Proteins

Basically, genes make proteins. That is their job. Here is how a protein is made: A molecule inside the cell "unzips" the DNA (like

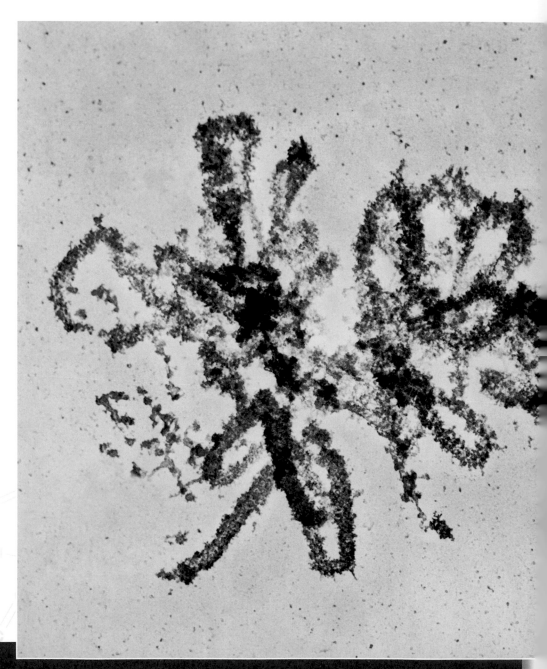

Scientists study lampbrush chromosomes, which are found in the immature egg cells of amphibians and birds, to understand how other chromosomes, including those of humans, operate.

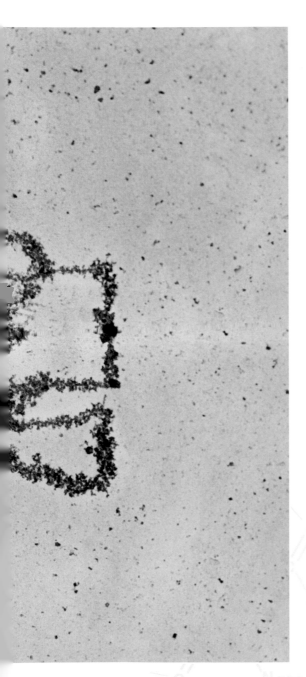

slicing the ladder down the middle of its rungs). The molecule copies one strand of the unraveled DNA into a similar chemical called messenger ribonucleic acid (mRNA), like a photocopy. This process is called transcription. The DNA strands rejoin, and the mRNA travels out of the cell's nucleus and into the cytoplasm. Next, translation happens. A chemical called a ribosome translates the three-letter words from the mRNA into one of twenty possible amino acids. These form a chain. When the chain is complete, it folds in a unique way. Now it is a protein.

There are only twenty different amino acids. But the four letters of the DNA alphabet can combine to form far more than twenty three-letter words. Some three-letter words are instructions for the same amino acid. For instance, CGC, CGA, and CGG are all instructions for the amino acid arginine, just as, in the English alphabet, cap and hat mean the same thing. The human body has about twenty

Svetlana Pankratova has the longest legs of any woman in the world. They are 4 feet, 4 inches (1.32 meters) long. He Pingping, 2 feet, 5 inches (.74 m) tall, is the world's smallest man. He was born with primordial dwarfism.

thousand to twenty-five thousand genes, but more than 120,000 proteins. Genes make, on average, three different proteins by splicing together different exons.

You can learn more facts about the genome in the following chapters. In the meantime, here's something to think about: We share 98 percent of our genome with chimpanzees. Our genome is also 50 percent the same as a banana's genome. How can this be? A banana isn't even an animal.

It's because the mechanisms for replicating DNA, making cells, making nutrients—basically, making and sustaining life— are the same no matter what the animal or plant is. These mechanisms worked for our earliest

Nature vs. Nurture: It's No Contest

Which is more important, nature or nurture? In other words, does our environment shape who we are and what we look like, or is it already set in stone by our DNA? Nature refers to genes. Nurture concerns upbringing, friends, nutrition, and other factors in the environment. The truth is, nurture and nature are not at odds. They are intertwined. Genes are designed to adapt to the environment—and maybe even to create the environment.

In the book Genome, Matt Ridley theorizes that the human genome has evolved to allow children to nurture their natural talents. A mechanically intelligent teenage girl, for instance, may start fixing cars. As she fixes more cars, the intelligence she was born with becomes stronger. Likewise, a boy interested in helping people will spend his time talking to people, making him more people smart. He might become a counselor.

According to this theory, a baby is not born with a certain nature and then molded by his or her environment. Instead, the baby grows up and molds the environment to fit his or her nature.

ancestors, and they work for humans, too. Therefore, they haven't changed.

Humans are 99.9 percent similar to each other. Chimps are four or five times more diverse as a species than we are. This is true for several reasons:

- *Homo sapiens* are a newer species, only about two hundred thousand years old.
- Humans had a small founding population and dwindled to a small group (possibly around two thousand total humans!) during the ice age. This is called a bottleneck.
- Human genes have been successful, so not much variation has built up.

Compared side by side, two genomes could differ by one in every thousandth letter. Considering humans have about three billion letters in our genome, two people sitting next to each other could have three million differences. These variations are called SNPs (pronounced "snips"). They account for many genetic differences among people. They also tell the story of our human ancestry.

The History of Genetics and the Human Genome Project

In the history of genetics, or the study of genes, many scientists have been ahead of their time, sometimes to the point of nobody knowing what they were talking about and everybody thinking they were insane. For instance, in the 1800s, Gregor Mendel, a monk who experimented with pea plants, discovered that offspring isn't simply a blend of two parents' traits. A spotted black-and-white cat is not simply a product of a black cat and a white cat breeding, but rather a mixture of particles carried by the parents. For decades, Mendel went unrecognized in the science community. Eventually, those particles became an accepted scientific fact. We now know them as genes. For this reason, Gregor Mendel is referred to today as the "Father of Genetics."

Then in 1892, a Swiss doctor named Friedrich Miescher theorized that DNA was an alphabet that determined heredity. Nobody believed him. Archibald Garrod theorized, in 1909, that genes made proteins. However, people didn't think DNA was that important.

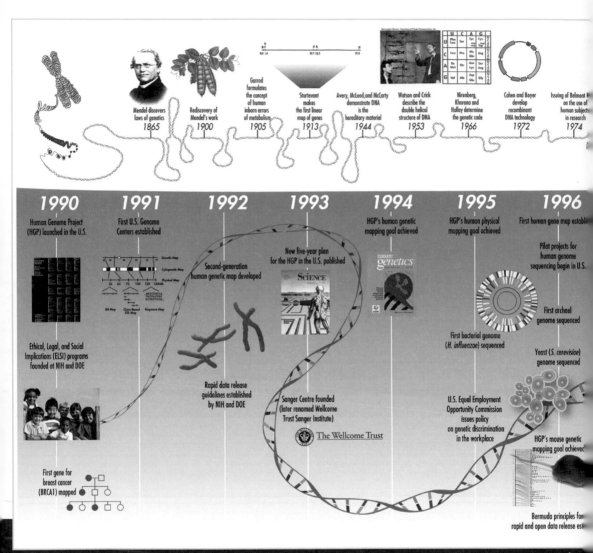

The following is a timeline of major discoveries in genetics:

Mendel discovers laws of genetics 1865

Rediscovery of Mendel's work 1900

Garrod formulates the concept of human inborn errors of metabolism 1905

Sturtevant makes the first linear map of genes 1913

Avery, McLeod, and McCarty demonstrate DNA is the hereditary material 1944

Watson and Crick describe the double helical structure of DNA 1953

Nirenberg, Khorana and Holley determine the genetic code 1966

Cohen and Boyer develop recombinant DNA technology 1972

Issuing of Belmont Report on the use of human subjects in research 1974

1990
Human Genome Project (HGP) launched in the U.S.

Ethical, Legal, and Social Implications (ELSI) programs founded at NIH and DOE

First gene for breast cancer (BRCA1) mapped

1991
First U.S. Genome Centers established

1992
Second-generation human genetic map developed

Rapid data release guidelines established by NIH and DOE

1993
New five-year plan for the HGP in the U.S. published

Sanger Centre founded (later renamed Wellcome Trust Sanger Institute)

The Wellcome Trust

1994
HGP's human genetic mapping goal achieved

1995
HGP's human physical mapping goal achieved

First bacterial genome (H. influenzae) sequenced

U.S. Equal Employment Opportunity Commission issues policy on genetic discrimination in the workplace

1996
First human gene map establi[shed]

Pilot projects for human genome sequencing begin in U.S.

First archael genome sequenced

Yeast (S. cerevisiae) genome sequenced

HGP's mouse genetic mapping goal achieve[d]

Bermuda principles for rapid and open data release est[ablished]

Unraveling the genome has been a long and winding road. Even after all of the research that has been done, scientists continue to learn more every day.

One problem was that genetics and evolution seemed to be at odds. If genes were passed on from parents, how could subsequent generations be so vastly different from their ancestors? In 1927, Hermann Joseph Muller found the answer. He discovered that X-rays

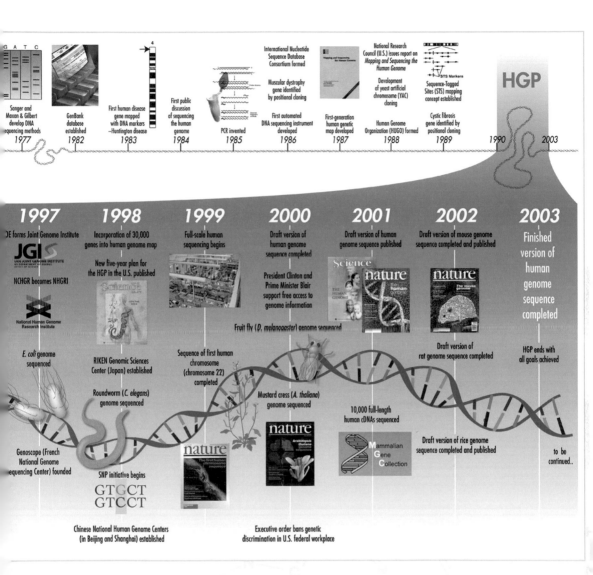

could artificially mutate genes. That meant genes could be broken down into multiple parts—what we now know as the nucleotide bases A, C, G, and T. These bases can be switched around, deleted, and even duplicated, resulting in mutation, which is the catalyst for evolution. For example, if a gene contains a code CCA, for the amino acid proline, and the first C is replaced by a G, this results in the GCA that codes for an entirely different amino acid, alanine.

This could greatly disturb the structure and function of the protein that a gene codes for. Not all mutations are negative, however. Sometimes they have no effect, sometimes they make a better protein than the original, and sometimes their effects are disastrous.

In the early 1950s, two scientists, James Watson and Francis Crick, together discovered the structure of DNA. They learned that DNA contained a code for building proteins. In short, they realized that DNA was the recipe for life.

By 1965, scientists understood how this code worked. However, decoding sequences was time-consuming. To find a gene related to a disease, scientists would examine a clump of DNA and write down a few hundred letters every day. It took around ten years to find the gene mutation that caused cystic fibrosis, around fifteen years to find just one of the breast cancer genes, and around twenty years to find the Huntington's mutation.

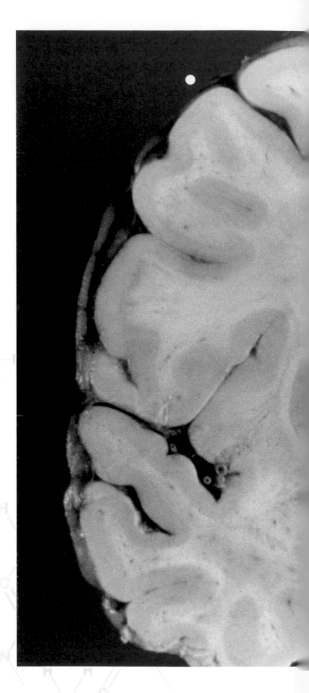

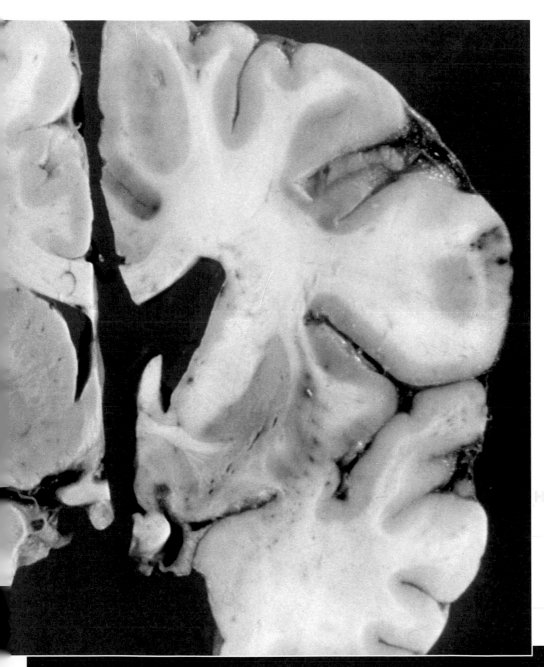

The brain on the left is healthy. The brain on the right, affected by Huntington's disease, has caudate atrophy. The caudate is shrinking, leaving an empty space that, in this picture, forms the shape of a butterfly wing.

Then a machine was invented that could decode one thousand letters every second. The publicly funded National Human Genome Research Institute announced in 1990 that it would map the entire human genome in fifteen years. The process would be called the Human Genome Project. Craig Venter, who owned the private company Celera Genomics, said in 1998 that he would map the genome in three years. The race was on.

The Human Genome Project

The Human Genome Project and the Celera project were different in several ways. The Human Genome Project was funded by the government and carried out by scientists from universities and government departments. They published their findings on the Web, believing the information should be free so that scientists could develop medicine and treatments. The genome they sequenced was a composite of people randomly chosen from the city of Buffalo, New York. They mapped the genome first and then sequenced it methodically.

The Celera project was privately funded and staffed. They didn't publish their findings, but they used those published on the Web by the Human Genome Project. This gave Celera an advantage but was legal, as the information was public. Celera based its genome on five

Craig Venter (left), former president Bill Clinton (center), and Francis Collins (right) announced on June 26, 2000, that Celera and the international Human Genome Project had both finished the initial sequence of the human genome.

people: two Caucasians, one Hispanic, one African American, and one person of Chinese descent. Celera randomly divided the genome, sequenced it, and then put it back together. This was called the shotgun approach.

The race ended up being a tie. In June 2000, U.S. President Bill Clinton announced that both groups had produced a first draft of the genome. He called it the greatest map ever created by humankind. It teaches us

Genome Map Quest: Francis Collins and Craig Venter

As a professor of internal medicine and genetics at the University of Michigan, Francis Collins led teams that discovered gene mutations for several diseases, including cystic fibrosis. He took charge of the publicly funded National Human Genome Research Institute in 1993, heading the Human Genome Project, which was to sequence the entire genome by 2005.

After serving as a U.S. Navy corpsman in Vietnam, Craig Venter attended college and graduate school. He then worked for the National Institutes of Health. While there, he used new machinery and developed faster ways to read genes. He started the Institute for Genomic Research. This nonprofit developed the shotgun technique of sequencing the genome. In 1998, Venter founded Celera Genomics and said the company would decode the human genome by 2001.

Collins sped up the Human Genome Project. He focused on finishing a first draft and filling in the details later. He funneled resources to the largest research institutes working on the project. Collins and Venter feuded bitterly. Then at the urging of President Clinton, they announced together in 2000 that they had completed a first draft of the human genome at the same time. Both will be remembered for cracking the code of life.

about our past, as our genes tell the story of our evolution and how we populated the earth. It has led to new disease treatments and will lead to new cures.

To most people, this is the best promise of the project. You might have a friend or family member for whom a genetic mutation has caused a debilitating or deadly disease. What if that gene could be changed? In this way, the Human Genome Project has offered hope for many people.

In addition to hope, the mapping of the genome gave surprising insights into our DNA. Scientists had guessed we'd have 150,000 genes. In fact, we only have twenty thousand to twenty-five thousand genes. The single-celled *Amoeba dubia* has a genome about two hundred times bigger than that of humans. This shows the size of the genome is unrelated to the complexity of the organism.

We also learned that one disease can occur in different people because of several different mutated genes. That is why different treatments work for different people. As scientists come to understand genes and disease better, they will tailor treatments according to patients' genes. The genome is like a universe inside each of us: It is full of discoveries yet to be made.

CHAPTER three

The Chromosomes

Twenty-three chromosome pairs are located in the nucleus of each of a person's cells. Scientists have numbered these chromosomes from largest to smallest. However, due to an early mistake, twenty-one is actually smaller than twenty-two. The sex chromosomes, X and Y are numbered twenty-three. Y is the smallest chromosome. X lies, in size, between seven and eight. Women have two X chromosomes. Men have one X and one Y.

The human genome is not necessarily organized. Unrelated genes cluster on the chromosomes, and genes that contribute to one trait are on different chromosomes. Our sense of smell, for instance, has one thousand genes scattered throughout the genome. Only 40 percent are functional, probably because we no longer rely on smell as much as our ancestors did.

It's no coincidence that humans have two pairs of chromosomes. Everyone receives a copy from each parent, which will be discussed in chapter four. Having two copies of a gene can be beneficial. If one gene is faulty, the working gene can take its place. This isn't always the case. In dominant diseases, one faulty gene causes a

Color blindness is more common in boys because the gene mutation occurs on the X chromosome. Since males have one X and one Y chromosome, the genes on the X chromosome do not have pairs that can override gene mutations.

problem. Also, since boys have just one X chromosome, a recessive gene on this chromosome can be expressed. That is why some genetic conditions, such as color blindness, are more common in men than women.

In news stories, genes are often linked to diseases, personality traits, or intelligence. These genes are the celebrities of the genome. However, most genes do ordinary, but important, jobs. They are the recipes for proteins that make up the body and allow it to function normally.

It's understandable that people have a greater interest in the more widely discussed genes. Understanding disease-related genes may lead to new treatments. And most people would like to know why they are good at math or bad at it, shy or friendly, cautious or impulsive. Is it in their genes? Or does their environment shape them? Both do to some extent. Below are two interesting genes and the chromosomes where you'll find them.

Are Stress and Grammar Genetic?

Language is a learned instinct. When humans are babies, they listen to people. Eventually, they speak—not just words, but whole sentences. As they get older, they get better at speaking in sentences. A three-year-old child might say, "My want ice cream. Chocolate." At age six, that same child might ask, "May I have a scoop of chocolate ice cream?" This is known as grammar.

Some scientists think the *FOXP2* gene on chromosome 7 helps people learn grammar. When this gene is abnormal, people of average or above-average intelligence have difficulty absorbing grammar rules. This is called specific language impairment (SLI). Say a person with SLI was given a new kind of candy called a Lemon Snap. If, next, they were given two, they would call them "two Lemon Snap," not "two Lemon Snaps." They'd have to learn the plural separately, as if, when plural, the candy had a new name.

Stress releases cortisol in the brain, triggering a weakened immune system. Worrying that something bad might happen releases cortisol, as if the bad thing has already happened.

People with SLI can learn grammar but only by memorizing it. It doesn't just "click" like it does for most people.

This shows that language may involve more than having intelligence and the mouth coordination to form words. It may also have

Chromosomal Conditions and Down Syndrome

More than half of all early miscarriages are due to a chromosomal abnormality. However, many babies are born with less or more than forty-six chromosomes. Depending on which chromosome is tripled or reduced to one, the condition can cause mild to severe physical or mental disabilities. A baby girl born with just one X chromosome may have Turner syndrome, which can result in slow growth, delayed puberty, and heart abnormalities. A child with an extra eighteenth chromosome has Edwards syndrome. The baby may die within a week. Those that survive to childhood or their teen years deal with severe medical problems and developmental disabilities.

The most commonly occurring chromosomal condition is Down syndrome, in which a baby is born with a third copy of the twenty-first chromosome. For this reason, Down syndrome is also known as trisomy 21. One in every eight hundred babies born in the United States is born with Down syndrome, and they typically have mild to moderate learning disabilities, developmental delays, and distinguishing physical characteristics. With early intervention and schooling tailored to their needs, children with Down syndrome often finish high school and go on to work full time or even attend college.

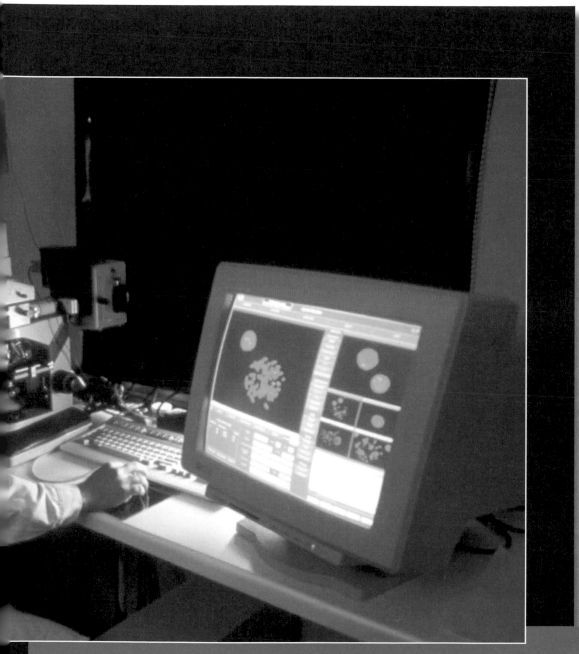

This geneticist is viewing the chromosomes of a fetus that has Down syndrome, as indicated by the three copies of chromosome 21. Some pregnant women opt to have this genetic test performed while pregnant.

to do with a gene that allows people to "hear" grammar rules and copy them.

Have you noticed that some people are stressed out by the smallest things, while others can handle big problems amazingly well? Some people are more genetically susceptible to stress than others. When something out of our control happens—such as a car wreck, a breakup with a boyfriend or girlfriend, or a family crisis—a gene called *CYP17*, one of the many genes involved with stress responses, makes an enzyme that converts cholesterol to several hormones, including cortisol. Having a lot of cortisol in the body means a person is under stress. Cortisol changes the configuration of the brain. It makes the ears, nose, and eyes more sensitive. It lessens the number of white blood cells, making a person more susceptible to sickness and disease. Research suggests that some laid-back people either produce or react to cortisol to a lesser extent than their high-strung counterparts.

The good news is that even in high-stress situations, people can do something about it—not on the inside, but on the outside. While a person may not be able to change his or her genes, he or she can change an environment and how to respond to it. For instance, if students dislike school, they might not be able to transfer, but they can take classes they enjoy, seek out friends who are nice, and be active in after-school activities.

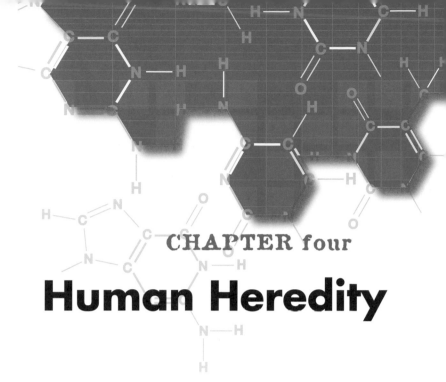

CHAPTER four

Human Heredity

Genes are passed down from parent to child. It happens like this:
A regular cell (with forty-six chromosomes, or two sets of twenty-three) goes through meiosis. During meiosis, the chromosomes swap
genetic information, and the cell divides. Finally, each reproductive
cell, or gamete, whether a sperm or an egg, is left with just twenty-three chromosomes. These chromosomes are a unique and random
mixture of the mother's genes or the father's genes. They may include
genes that were not expressed in the mother or father, but will be in
the child. In fact, every man or woman can produce eight million
possible gametes. Together, they can create sixty-four trillion different possible children (which is why two siblings may be very
different from each other).

When the nucleus of the sperm (gamete one) meets the nucleus of
the egg (gamete two), they fuse to form a new cell, the zygote. The
zygote has forty-six chromosomes—twenty-three from each parent.
These chromosomes hold all of your genes. The zygote duplicates
several times, going through the stages of embryonic development.
Finally, it is a baby with ten trillion cells, which will become a

When genes from the mother and father are shuffled, they can create sixty-four trillion different possible children. This explains why siblings are sometimes very different.

grown-up with one hundred trillion cells. Each of these cells, with a couple of exceptions, carries all the chromosome pairs—the entire genome. However, some genes are never expressed. For instance, one in thirty-one Americans is a genetic carrier for cystic fibrosis. Unless both parents are carriers, a baby has no chance of getting the disease. However, the child might be a carrier like his or her mom or dad.

A genotype refers to a person's entire genetic makeup. A phenotype is the part of the genome that is expressed—in other words, what you see. What determines which genes are expressed and which aren't? Lots of factors.

Some genes are dominant or recessive. If people inherit a gene from just one parent for a dominant disease, they will develop that disease. Huntington's is a dominant disease. On chromosome 4, one gene repeats the sequence

Is Crime in the Genes?

A so-called crime gene was found in a Dutch family. A pregnant woman asked her doctor if her child would be mentally retarded, like many men in her family. The doctor learned that the men were not, in fact, mentally disabled but were violent instead. They had a single point mutation on the gene MAO on the X chromosome. Typically, this gene breaks down serotonin, another neurotransmitter in the brain involved in regulating impulsivity and inhibition of responses. When this gene doesn't function well, it can impair the fight-or-flight response and the response to stress. It can cause aggression, but it doesn't always.

The mutation is rare and definitely not the cause of all crime. Instead of relying on genetic causes to explain crime, researchers recommend focusing on social factors, such as childcare and education.

CAG. If this happens thirty-five times or less, the person is fine. If it happens forty times or more, he or she will get the disease. The more times it's repeated, the earlier the patient will get it and the more severe the symptoms will be. (At least one other gene also affects the age of onset.) Huntington's appears in adulthood and causes depression, loss of balance, hallucinations, delusions, and ultimately death. If a parent has Huntington's, the odds are fifty-fifty that a child will, too. Scientists are trying to find a cure.

One example of a recessive disease is Tay-Sachs. It, too, is devastating. Afflicted babies start out healthy, but lose brain function and die by about age six. Unlike dominant diseases in which one dominant gene results in disease, a person must inherit two recessive genes to develop a disease. If just one parent is a carrier of the Tay-Sachs gene, the baby has no chance of getting the disease. If each parent is a carrier, the baby has a 25 percent chance of inheriting the disease by getting a recessive gene from each carrier parent.

Multi-Gene Traits and the Environment

Other genes are additive, meaning they combine to create a certain trait. Take height, for instance. It is affected by about one hundred genes. The genes inherited from a mother and those inherited from a father combine to create a person's height. In boys, a gene on the Y chromosome increases that height by about 3 inches (.076 meters). A family might have one boy who is 6 feet, 2 inches (1.87 m) tall and another who is 5 feet, 7 inches (1.69 m) tall. This is because each parent passed on genes to the child randomly. With the shorter son, those genes came from relatives who were shorter. The taller son's genes came from relatives who were taller.

Additive genes make up many traits, including several personality characteristics. If a person tends to take risks, that may be due to about eleven different genes, including DRD4 on chromosome 11. In the middle of this gene, a sequence of letters repeats eleven times.

Personality traits can be affected, in part, by your genes. Risk-seeking is about 40 percent heritable. Environmental factors—such as friends and cultural trends—play a larger role.

The larger the number of repeats, the more ineffectively a person's brain captures dopamine, a neurotransmitter or chemical involved in motivation and pleasure. That means the person needs to do something adventurous to get the same dopamine buzz that others get from doing ordinary things. Risk-seeking is only about 40 percent heritable, however. That means even if a person is genetically inclined toward risk-taking, he or she may be influenced by environmental factors like friends and upbringing, and never take risks. Or he or she might take calculated risks, such as quitting a job to start a business, but not foolish ones, such as driving recklessly.

Personality traits may be hereditary in part, but they're not set in stone. People's environment and even their self-perception play a role. Many learning disabilities are genetic. However, as these students learn study skills, they often wind up getting better grades than those who don't have a disability. Some people may be prone to stress. But by exercising, surrounding themselves with good friends, and choosing enjoyable careers, they can limit how often their cortisone-releasing genes go into overdrive. Shyness is probably genetic, but once people accept their shyness as part of their genetic makeup, they usually feel more comfortable around people.

Some traits might seem like they're in the genes. If everybody in a family likes barbecue, it must be genetic! Actually, it's not. Rather, it's part of the family's culture. Culture is a strong factor in who a person is. Look at the Vikings of Scandinavia. A thousand years ago, they were ruthless warriors. Today's Scandinavian people inherited genes from their Viking ancestors, but Scandinavia is a pacifist region. Their genes didn't change. (Not enough time passed to make that possible.) Their culture did.

CHAPTER five

Human History

As humans, we are the only species on earth that can understand our own genome. And to think, one of our earliest ancestors was a worm. Five hundred thirty million years ago, we descended from a type of flatworm. We were able to evolve into new species—with arms and legs—thanks, in part, to our HOX genes. HOX genes are laid out head to toe and dictate how the fetus develops in the womb and which genes are expressed and when. They also help species evolve into new species by regulating gene expression, or which genes are "on" and which are "off."

Eventually, we became primates. We shared a common ancestor with chimpanzees six to seven million years ago. Chimpanzees have twenty-four chromosome pairs compared to our twenty-three. At some point, our second and third chromosomes fused. Amazingly, our DNA is 99 percent the same as chimpanzees. However, since we have three billion units, that leaves us with thirty million differences. In everyday life, an obvious difference is that chimpanzees do not have speech (except for a little sign language in some labs).

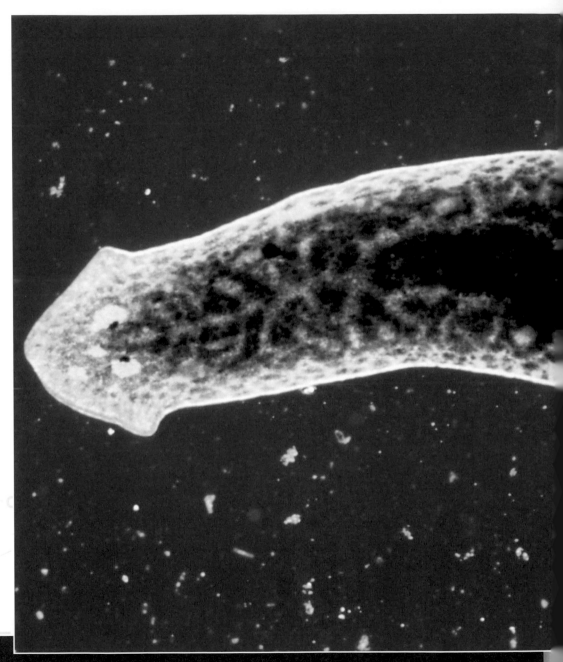

Grandmother, is that you? Humans descended from a type of flatworm, which may have looked like this turbellarian coldwater flatworm. HOX genes, in part, allowed us to evolve into new species.

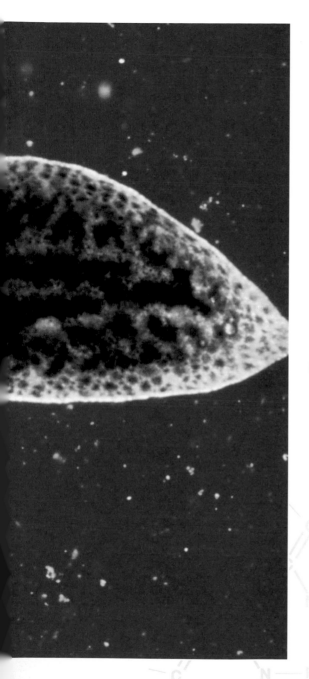

The primate family tree gave birth to several species; our branch evolved into *Homo sapiens*. About 195,000 years ago, all humans living today shared a common female ancestor known as Mitochondrial Eve. She wasn't the only woman living back then. However, she was the only one to pass on her mitochondrial DNA to future generations of women. Mitochondria are structures within cells that produce energy. Interestingly, they contain a small loop of DNA. During reproduction, mitochondrial DNA from the male's sperm is left behind. As a result, we all carry our mother's mitochondrial DNA. For this reason, mitochondrial DNA can be used to trace generations back to our common ancestors and the origin of our species. The last shared male ancestor, Scientific Adam, lived sixty thousand years ago. He passed on his genetic markers through the male Y chromosome to future generations of men. Adam and Eve

Because Africa is the most genetically diverse continent in the world, two of these children could be more different from each other than they would be from someone living on the other side of the world.

both lived in Africa, but obviously weren't a couple.

About 130,000 years ago, an ice age turned Africa from lush land into a desert. According to many scientists, the entire human population dwindled to about two thousand—the size of the population of some high schools. This caused a genetic bottleneck resulting in gene mutation spreading through the population faster, speeding up evolution, and giving birth to a human species that now has very little genetic diversity. The wildebeest in Kenya alone have twice as much genetic variation as the six billion humans all over the world. Among humans, Africa is the most genetically diverse continent in the world because our species has been living there the longest. Two people from the same village in Africa could be more different from each other than they would from someone living outside of Africa.

By about fifty thousand years ago, language had

developed, probably, in part, due to the *FOXP2* gene. Some of our ancestors migrated out of Africa. Our genome tells the history of this migration. About every ten thousand years, a mutation occurs on mitochondrial DNA. If two people share all but one mutation, their closest ancestor lived ten thousand years ago. Native Americans share a common ancestor with a clan living in Siberia twenty thousand years ago. Other clans may have traveled to America, too, but only the descendants of one clan survived. Forty thousand years ago, Native Americans and Europeans shared a common ancestor in Central Asia.

Natural Selection and Chance

Physical differences among *Homo sapiens* developed ten thousand years after the species left Africa. Genetic drift—or chance—played a role. Five clans may have set out for new land. Due to a difficult journey, harsh climate, and fierce predators, only one may have survived. That clan would have had certain genes that caused traits neither helpful nor harmful, such as red hair. Those traits would be prevalent in future generations.

Natural selection played a large role in the traits that humans developed. It works like this: A mutation causes a gene to either stop making proteins or make a protein with a different structure. This can be helpful, harmful, helpful and harmful, or have no effect. If the mutation boosts the number of offspring, it will spread through the population. This is natural selection. When a gene has more muta-tions in its coding region than in its noncoding region, natural selection probably influenced the genetic change.

As primates developed, natural selection helped them develop an upright gait, bigger brains, and some of the instincts that we still have today. Once *Homo sapiens* evolved and spread out around the planet, natural selection worked on individual groups of people. Consider milk. Most mammals can only drink milk (their mother's) as

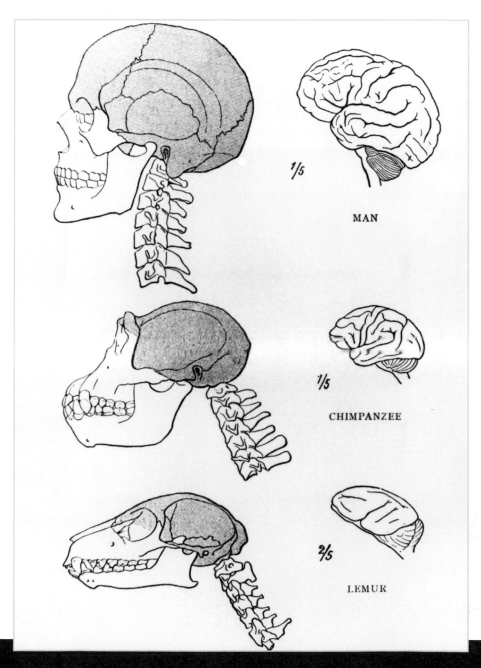

1/5

MAN

1/5

CHIMPANZEE

2/5

LEMUR

As some species of primates developed, natural selection resulted in larger brains. A human has a larger brain than a chimpanzee, which has a larger brain than a lemur. All of these primates share a common ancestor.

babies. Later, their bodies do not produce the lactase that breaks it down. Thousands of years ago, cattle herders developed a mutation to a gene called *LCT*, which allowed them to digest milk. The mutation happened randomly, but the extra calories resulted in milk drinkers having more children. (People who were not cattle herders may have also had this mutation, but because they didn't have milk available, it didn't result in more children.) Today, 70 percent of the cattle herders' descendants can drink milk, as opposed to only 30 percent of the people who do not descend from the herders.

Was Your Great Grandfather a Neanderthal?

When Homo sapiens *left Africa and spread throughout the world, they likely encountered other species of humans, including the Neanderthals in Europe. For years, scientists debated whether Europeans mated with Neanderthals, in which case, modern Europeans would have some Neanderthal genes. With knowledge of the genome, scientists were able to test that theory. Looking at the mitochondrial DNA of Neanderthal remains found in Croatia, scientists didn't see genetic markers that would indicate interbreeding between species. They have since mapped the Neanderthal genome, confirming that Homo sapiens and Neanderthals didn't mate on a large scale.*

However, archaeological evidence of tools and burial sites shows that Neanderthals were similar to our ancestors in intelligence and culture. The Neanderthal genome indicates that they, too, had the FOXP2 gene, meaning they probably talked. So why didn't the two species hit it off? Perhaps they viewed each other as separate species (which they were) and, thus, too different. Or they simply might not have encountered each other that often, as the number of Neanderthals was dwindling at the time.

Skin color changed for a similar reason. Our primate ancestors lost body hair so that they wouldn't overheat. They were pale underneath. In sunny Africa, this not only would have caused severe sunburns and skin cancer, but also folic acid imbalances, making men infertile and causing babies to be born with birth defects. Natural selection caused people in sunny areas to have dark skin. Those with lighter skin did not survive the harshness of their sunny environment, and thus could not reproduce and pass along their light-skinned genes to subsequent generations. Likewise, when some humans migrated north thousands of years ago, their dark skin caused problems. They absorbed less vitamin D. This led to rickets, a condition that affects bone development, and other diseases. In these areas, light skin became a helpful gene mutation.

Today, people can wear sunscreen to avoid too much sun exposure and take vitamin D supplements to cope with too little sun. We can adapt to harsh environments by using heating, cooling, and water irrigation. We can immunize against childhood diseases. These human innovations may influence natural selection.

CHAPTER six

Genetic Diseases

Every time a cell divides, the DNA in the nucleus replicates. During this duplication, all three billion letters of the genome are copied and about three mistakes occur. Many of these mutations make no difference. Either they occur on DNA that doesn't encode for proteins, or the new gene is equally capable of making a protein. Other times, the mutations are helpful, as in the case of the "milk gene." But sometimes, one wrong letter can have tragic results. When errors occur in somatic cells, which do not produce gametes, the mistakes are not passed on to future generations. When they occur in germ cells, which produce gametes for reproduction (sperm and egg), the mutated genes become hereditary. Errors in single genes are responsible for more than four thousand hereditary diseases, including sickle-cell anemia, Tay-Sachs, and cystic fibrosis.

Cystic fibrosis is the most common inherited fatal disease in the United States, with one in thirty-one people being carriers. It is a recessive disease. The cystic fibrosis gene leads to a defective protein that was supposed to regulate chloride and sodium in lung cells and other organ cells. With the protein broken, a salt

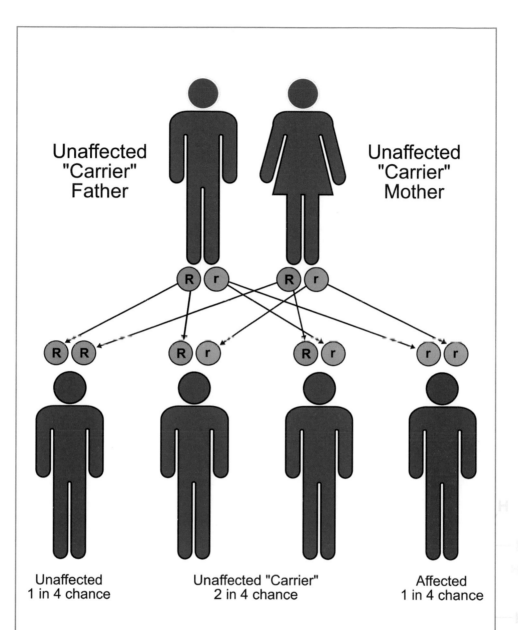

Unaffected
"Carrier"
Father

Unaffected
"Carrier"
Mother

R r   R r

R R   R r   R r   r r

Unaffected
1 in 4 chance

Unaffected "Carrier"
2 in 4 chance

Affected
1 in 4 chance

Two carriers of a gene mutation that causes a recessive disease have a one in four chance of passing both genes on to a child. If only one parent is a carrier, there is no chance of the child having the disease.

imbalance causes mucus in the lungs to thicken. It clogs the airways, making it difficult to breathe and causing infections. In the 1950s, patients with cystic fibrosis typically died in early childhood. With new treatments, the life expectancy is 37.4. However, that depends on the severity of the disease in the patient. When a couple knows that one of them is a carrier (because a sibling had cystic fibrosis), they may seek genetic counseling prior to having a baby or once the woman is pregnant. They face tough decisions on what to do with the information. One day the genome could provide a fix for these diseases.

With increasing knowledge of the genome, a cure for cystic fibrosis seems likely. Through gene therapy, doctors have loaded a working copy of the CF gene into a virus incapable of causing disease but still able to enter cells. This virus was used as a delivery system, or vector, for getting the working gene into the lung cells of cystic fibrosis patients. After injecting the virus into the lungs, they hoped it would enter the patient's lung cells and insert the working gene into the existing cells where it would be expressed. Gene therapy hasn't worked for cystic fibrosis so far. One problem is that lung viruses don't spread fast enough. Scientists are now trying to evolve viruses in the lab so that they will spread faster, which should make gene therapy more effective. They're also studying a gene that lessons the severity of the disease, which could lead to new treatments and a longer lifespan for these patients. You'll read more about future disease treatments and cures in the last chapter.

Genes can affect a person's health positively, too. If members of a family live to old age, they may have genes that inhibit the production of free radicals, preventing cells from getting damaged by oxygen. They may also have long repeats at the beginning of each chromosome. When the genome is copied as cells divide throughout a person's life, these repeats tend to get left off. When they vanish, important letters eventually get erased. The longer a person's repeats,

Genetic Testing: One Community Eradicates a Childhood Disease

Tay-Sachs results from one letter in three billion being wrong. It is one of the most tragic diseases that a child can have. A mutated gene affects the structure of the enzyme hexosaminidase A (HexA), which should break down a fatty substance in the brain. Instead, the substance accumulates in nerve cells. The nerves cannot transmit signals. Parents see the baby change. He loses his ability to laugh. Soon he can't move. Even as he grows older, he needs to be cared for like a baby. At about six years old, the child dies.

Among the Ashkenazi Jewish population, one in twenty-seven people are carriers. A recessive disease, both parents need to be carriers for their child to get it. Rabbi Joseph Ekstein watched four of his eleven children suffer from the disease. He started a program to prevent it from recurring in his Orthodox Jewish community of Williamsburg, Brooklyn.

In this community, a matchmaker helps families arrange marriages. Through Ekstein's program, part of the matchmaking process now involves blood testing for the Tay-Sachs gene. If both people in a potential couple have the gene, the matchmaker doesn't go forward with the match. Today, no child is born with Tay-Sachs in the rabbi's neighborhood, and the program has expanded elsewhere.

the less this process damages his or her genes. In this way, living a long life can be hereditary.

Do Diseases Have a Good Side?

At some point, spiritual people may ask their parents or religious leaders, "Why did God make diseases?" There's no question that diseases can have tragic results. But here's something to consider: Historically, they might have had no effect. And though we are taught to think that diseases are bad, some might have even helped people survive.

Diabetes, for instance, is an epidemic in America, where food is plentiful. In the past, however, it may have helped people survive famine because they were better able to store starches and sugars.

Asthma may be another example. Several genes have been linked to asthma, and the disease varies between men and women and among ethnic groups. On the whole, asthma has increased in recent years. There are several theories to explain this. One has to do with sanitation. Genes linked to asthma produce histamines that flush harmful parasites from the stomach. In the Stone Age, sanitation was poor. People who could flush worms from their guts had the advantage of not getting sick.

Today, however, we have good sanitation. The histamines (which some believe may also be stimulated by childhood vaccinations) aren't fighting worms and therefore go into overdrive, fighting dust mites and other allergens. These allergic reactions can lead to asthma, a dangerous condition if left untreated. In the Stone Age, being allergic to dust was no big deal. In their temporary homes, dust didn't accumulate. So people with "asthma" were the healthy ones.

On the flip side, some diseases that are minor problems today could have been fatal in the past. Thousands of years ago, nearsighted hunters wouldn't have seen nearby dangers. Lactose-intolerant cow herders would have faced starvation during times of famine.

Keep in mind that everybody has the genes that are linked to diseases. Only the altered genes cause disease. Some mutations can

Dr. Francis Collins, who headed the international Human Genome Project, has researched gene therapy for cystic fibrosis, among other diseases.

cause one disease and prevent another. Often, the disease that is prevented used to be an epidemic. Tay-Sachs is most common among the Ashkenazi Jewish population. Being a carrier for Tay-Sachs makes a person more resistant to tuberculosis, which, in the past, was a dangerous epidemic for people, including Ashkenazi Jews, living in crowded cities. Today, tuberculosis is treatable.

Sickle-cell anemia is a disease in which red blood cells are sickle-shaped, clogging blood vessels and causing infections, organ damage, and chronic pain and fatigue. In the United States, the disease is most common among African Americans. One in twelve African Americans is a carrier, and one in five hundred is born with the condition. Being a carrier for sickle-cell anemia provides some resistance to malaria, a disease that has plagued sub-Saharan Africa. Malaria has been eliminated in the United States and could be eradicated worldwide with the preventative medicine available today.

In the United States, these resistances are not helpful. So there is no "good side" to the diseases. However, it explains why natural selection allowed the mutations to spread through generations.

CHAPTER seven

Ethics and the Genome

Leaders of the National Human Genome Research Institute knew that ethical issues would arise from the Human Genome Project. In 1990, they established ELSI, the Ethical, Legal, and Social Implications research program. It addresses such topics as intellectual property, genetic research methods, and genetics in health care. In May 2008, ELSI achieved an important goal when the Genetic Information Nondiscrimination Act became law. The act protects patients against employment or insurance discrimination based on their genetic information.

An ongoing ethical debate relating to the genome concerns intellectual property. Many companies are developing diagnostic tests and treatments based on genetic knowledge. Should they be able to patent a gene found in the human body?

At first glance, people probably would think not. What's next? Will they patent the eyeball? They didn't invent it. Nor did they invent human genes. But scientists can't simply look at a gene and declare it theirs. In order for it to be patented, it needs to be isolated and purified, and the scientists need to have a purpose for the patent—that the gene will be used to develop a diagnostic test, for instance. Second, patents make innovation financially possible. Research and development of gene-related tests and treatments costs money. Research companies and universities want to earn back the money they invested. Fearing that competitors will make the same product discourages research and development.

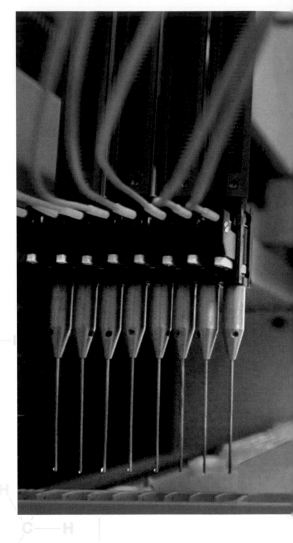

By the same token, too many patents may discourage research and development. Genes can be patented in multiple ways, including as segments and whole genes, and as genes and SNPs (mutated genes). Scientists wanting to research a genetic disease may find that the licensing fees are too expensive. Or they may worry that they will research a gene, only to learn halfway through that it has just been patented.

Then there is the patient's point of view. Gene patents can prevent patients from getting a cheaper diagnostic test or a second opinion on the test. That's what several cancer patients, women's health groups, pathologists, and researchers argued in a case brought by the American Civil Liberties Union (ACLU) and the Public Patent Foundation against Myriad Genetics in 2009. Myriad had

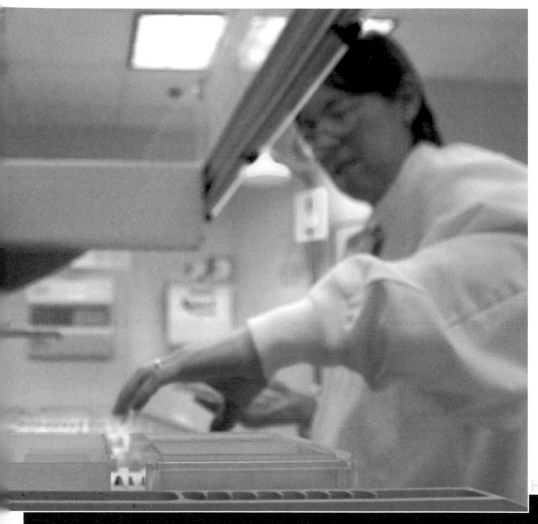

A worker at Myriad Genetics tests patient DNA samples. Myriad has created genetic tests for breast and ovarian cancers. To what extent companies should be able to patent genes, in the interest of developing genetic tests, continues to be debated.

patented two breast cancer gene mutations and the diagnostic test for them. Because of the patents, there were no other diagnostic tests available. The patent prevented other companies from creating better, faster, or cheaper tests, or researching other aspects of the gene. The ACLU said patenting genes essentially patents knowledge, and that limits freedom of speech. The result of the lawsuit remains to be seen.

As more genes are patented, and as tests for diseases look at multiple genes, it might be harder for scientists to get all the necessary patents to study a disease. Intellectual property will likely be a controversial topic in the genetics field for years to come.

Personal Ethics

Some genetic ethics involve more personal choices. Genetic tests for more than one thousand diseases are available to patients. Deciding whether to be tested (or have a child tested) forces people to make

Dr. Nancy Wexler is a leader in the study of Huntington's disease. She has worked with many families who carry the disease. It has touched her personally, too. She tested positive for Huntington's and her mother died of it.

tough decisions. For instance, should tests be provided for diseases that have no cure? What should a person do with the information, and how might it alter his or her life? This is particularly an issue in the case of diseases for which multiple genes play a role. If patients are told they have a gene associated with a particular deadly disease, but that this is no guarantee they will actually get the disease, will the information negatively impact their lives unnecessarily?

Huntington's tests have been available for a long time. In the case of dominant diseases like Huntington's, if the test is positive, nothing can be done about it. Some people don't want to know. A positive result would be too devastating. Others do want to know, however. Adults are free to request information about their own health. But what if a twelve-year-old wants to know if he or she has the CAG repeat that causes Huntington's? What if his or her parents want to know? In 1993, the Institute of Medicine's bioethics committee said it was inappropriate to test for genes in children unless that disease could be prevented, treated, or cured. In 2006, Nancy Wexler, a leader in the discovery of the Huntington's gene and who has Huntington's disease herself, spoke to the President's Council on Bioethics. She recommended that children not be tested for late-onset diseases that cannot be treated in childhood. She said they may spend years worrying, only to learn of a cure later in life. However, she said that while guidelines exist, labs don't always follow them.

Looking on the flip side, is it unethical not to test for some diseases? Rabbi Ekstein said it was unethical not to be tested for the Tay-Sachs gene prior to marriage. He argued: Why refuse a test that would save your baby from a harmful disease?

Testing for the health of a baby is a sensitive issue for people who may be carriers. Some people want to be tested before they conceive. However, if both the husband and the wife are carriers, they might still want to have children. Options include preimplantation genetic diagnosis (PGD). In this case, embryos are created in vitro

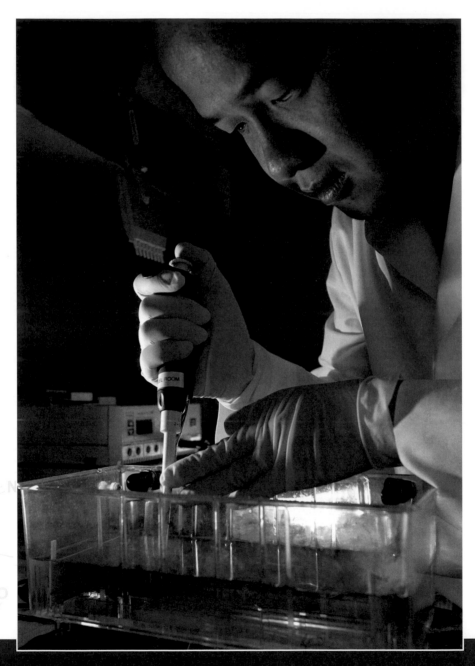

A scientist examines DNA samples for variations that would put the patient at risk for lung, prostate, breast, or colorectal cancer. As the genome is better understood, medical tests and treatments will likely become more personalized.

using the mother's egg and the father's sperm. The DNA of the early embryos is then tested for a genetic mutation that they are at risk for, such as the cystic fibrosis or Huntington's gene. Only the mutation-free embryos are implanted.

Discussion: Genetic Engineering

In the movie Gattaca, parents who can afford genetic engineering design their children to be athletic, smart, and healthy. Soon genetically unaltered people are discriminated against for their lack of perfection. The main character, Vincent, has to pretend to be genetically enhanced in order to be an astronaut.

Could this happen in the future? Geneticists say it's unlikely in the near future. Several genes influence a person's traits. How they interact is unknown. Altering a gene may cause unknown side effects. Also, children's experiences (nurture), affect how their genes operate.

But let's say that genetic engineering like this could happen. Should parents do it? They would be making decisions that their children might not make for themselves. On the other hand, nature currently makes decisions for children against their will.

Would parents seek genetically engineered children? Parents try to give their children a leg up. Would they select the best genome for their child, too? Or would this cross the moral line? In addition, there has been much debate over "positive" genetic engineering, or enhancement, and "negative" genetic engineering—correcting disease. While it is arguable that preventing a child from having a deadly disease like cystic fibrosis is ethical, is it also OK to make them taller? Being short is certainly not deadly, but some people argue that shorter people are at a disadvantage compared to taller people. Where do we draw the line?

Would genetically enhanced children really have an advantage? Would their "perfection" have any drawbacks? Or would they lead better lives? Would society suffer? Or could a generation with altered intelligence lead us to amazing new discoveries?

Other at-risk couples screen for genetic diseases after the woman is pregnant. If the fetus is carrying genes for a fatal disease, the couple faces a tough choice: Should they go through with the pregnancy?

Today, all pregnant women are routinely offered a screening for Down syndrome. But it is the woman's choice to be tested and, if the results are positive, to proceed with the pregnancy.

People have strong feelings about the ethics of testing fetuses. Their opinions might depend on their view of disabilities. If they think people with Down syndrome have a good quality of life, as many of them do, they might think a trisomy-21 screening test is unnecessary. If somebody in their family suffers from a painful disease, they might think genetic counseling or PGD is a good idea for couples at risk. Their opinion might depend on at what point they view an embryo as a full-fledged person. Immediately after conception (the joining of sperm and egg)? After implantation into the uterine wall? At the moment the woman feels the baby move? After the child is born?

In the end, it is up to the individual to make these difficult decisions. Doctors hope that, in the future, parents will be offered not only genetic tests for their children, but genetic cures as well.

CHAPTER eight

The Future

If the average person were given the parts list for a Boeing 747, would he or she be able to build the plane? Of course not. The person would have no idea of how things fit together. Also, he or she would only have the list, not the actual parts.

This is how scientists feel about the human genome. They have a list of genes. (In fact, everybody does. It's available for public viewing on the Internet.) But they don't know the function of every gene. They don't know how all the genes work together to build proteins. They don't fully understand how proteins work together to build humans. Mapping the genome was one of the biggest scientific accomplishments of all time. But it was only the first step.

Today, scientists are studying:

- How genomes vary among people. Haplogroups represent people who share similar variations in their genomes. Different groups may get diseases for different genetic reasons, for instance. Understanding these groups will help scientists tailor disease treatments for them.

This Yale University scientist examines a computerized display of human genes. They are studied using a small cartridge called a gene chip. The chip contains the entire human genome.

- The location, interaction, structure, and function of proteins, a study known as proteomics. Determining the structures of human proteins will be a bigger job than sequencing the genome. The genome sequence is linear. It can be read like a book. Proteins are three-dimensional. Studying proteins is important, however, as diseases may be curable through protein therapy.
- The physical structure of our genome. The DNA double helix is wrapped around protein molecules to form a nucleosome, which makes a thread called chromatin. When cells are copied, chromatin loops and coils to make chromosomes. Scientists believe that understanding the shape of our genome is an important part of the big picture.
- How genes are related to each other. Scientists are learning that even single gene diseases, such as cystic fibrosis, may be affected by different genes. This can lead to treatments.

As technology improves, new discoveries are happening faster. It took years for the first human genome to be mapped. The time later shrunk to months and then a week. Soon a new method called single-molecule, real-time (SMRT) sequencing could allow the human genome to be mapped in just fifteen minutes. As the process gets faster, it will become cheaper.

In the future, a doctor could have patients' genomes on file and advise them about what lifestyle choices may improve their health. For instance, for some people, such as those with genes that make them susceptible to heart disease, a diet that is low in cholesterol and fat is very important. Other people really don't have to worry about it, assuming they stay at a healthy weight.

For people already coping with a genetic disease, scientists are developing new treatments based on their knowledge of the genome.

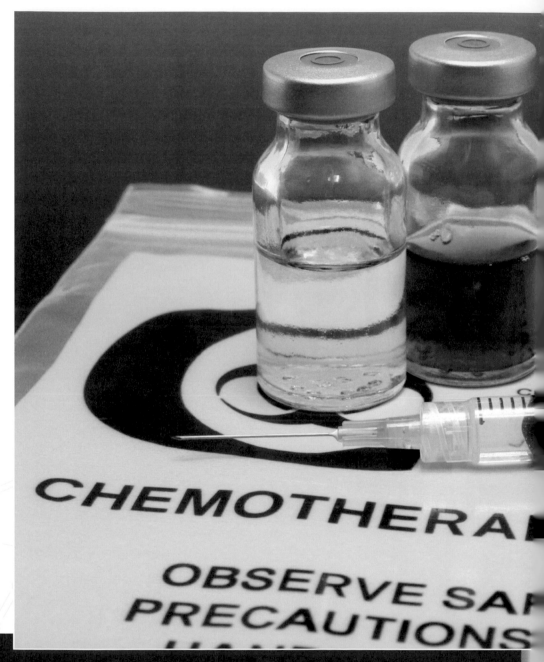

Chemotherapy fights cancer by damaging cells enough to alert the protein P53, which tells the cells to commit suicide. If the TP53 gene, which encodes P53, is damaged, chemotherapy won't work.

How the Genome Is Changing Medicine

Already, individualized medical tests and treatments are used for different types of breast cancer and other diseases. That individualization will grow. Not only will gene-specific treatments be more effective, they'll also have fewer side effects.

Knowledge of the genome will likely revolutionize cancer treatments. Cancer grows like this: If a gene called an oncogene is jammed on, and a tumor suppressor gene is jammed off, there is a threat of cancer as a cell grows and divides uncontrollably. This doesn't happen often. However, since our cells divide so much, cancer can result if it happens just once in one hundred billion times. At that point, the *TP53* gene on chromosome 17, which encodes protein P53, tells cancerous cells to commit suicide, a process known as apoptosis.

Ethical Clone Wars

Sometimes scientific discovery can outpace ethical decisions. Human cloning involves taking an egg cell, removing the nucleus, and replacing it with the nucleus of one of a person's body cells. The resulting cell would be grown into an embryo and implanted into a womb. Once born, the child would be like the adult's younger identical twin. Many people see this type of cloning as a nonissue because—legal and ethical concerns aside—not many people want to clone themselves.

The more heated debate concerns embryonic stem cell research. Technically, this involves cloning, even though the embryo is never implanted. Instead, stem cells are harvested from the blastocyst, which is an early embryonic stage. The stem cells are studied as potential cures for diseases.

Some people believe that an embryo at any stage, even before it is implanted in the uterine wall, is a person. They think that researchers are creating a human clone with rights and a soul and are destroying it. Proponents of stem cell research, on the other hand, believe the blastocyst is a collection of cells with disease-curing potential.

Lawmakers have struggled to keep up with the debate. For eight years, the U.S. government prevented researchers from using federal funds for embryonic stem cell research. In 2009, President Barack Obama lifted the ban.

People with one faulty *TP53* gene have a higher chance of getting cancer, as these uncontrollably dividing cells are not signaled appropriately to self-destruct.

Scientists used to think that radiation and chemotherapy treated cancer because it killed the cells by damaging their DNA. In fact, the damage isn't enough to kill the cells. It's only enough to alert P53, which tells the multiplying cells to dismantle themselves. If

TP53 is damaged, chemotherapy doesn't work because P53 can't order the cells to commit suicide. In the future, doctors may develop treatments in which P53 can more effectively order cancerous cells to dismantle.

Gene therapy offers another hope for curing diseases. It has effectively been used to treat children with severe combined immuno-deficiency (SCID). This condition once required children to live their entire lives in a germ-free bubble because SCID causes them to be exceptionally prone to infections that they cannot fight off. Now with gene therapy and other interventions, they can lead a more normal life. Scientists believe gene therapy will also work for diseases like Lou Gehrig's, Alzheimer's, and cystic fibrosis. It is a matter of discovering the right method for each disease.

Glossary

cell A small unit of protoplasm that usually has a nucleus containing an individual's entire genome, cytoplasm, and a membrane.

chromosomes The microscopic rods that form during meiosis and mitosis and contain DNA.

DNA (deoxyribonucleic acid) The chemical compound that contains instructions for building proteins.

dominant gene A gene that a person expresses if he or she inherits just one copy.

ELSI The research program created by the National Human Genome Research Institute to explore the ethical, legal, and social implications of human genome research.

gamete A sex cell, either a sperm or egg.

gene A string of nucleotide bases that gives instructions for making a protein.

gene therapy A disease treatment in which doctors insert a working copy of a gene into a harmless virus and infect the patient in hopes that the healthy gene cells will insert their code into the existing cells.

genetic drift The process by which genetic changes spread through a population due to chance.

genotype A person's entire collection of genes, expressed or not.

germ cell A cell that becomes a gamete.

Homo sapiens The only living species of humans.

Human Genome Project A government-funded program through which scientists mapped the human genome.

natural selection The process by which animals develop genetic mutations that result in higher birthrates, causing the mutation to spread throughout the population.

nucleotide bases The four chemicals that make up the DNA code; they are adenine, cytosine, guanine, and thymine. In groups of three, they make up "words" that are recipes for amino acids.

Glossary

phenotype The collection of genes that are expressed in an individual.

protein A chemical substance made up of amino acids. It provides the structure and facilitates the processes of living things.

recessive gene A gene requiring two copies, one from each parent, in order for it to be expressed.

ribosome Molecular machine that makes proteins out of amino acids.

RNA (ribonucleic acid) A long chain of nucleotides found in cells. Messenger RNA (mRNA) carries copies of DNA to the cell cytoplasm to be translated into amino acids.

somatic cell Any cell that does not become a gamete.

transcription The process of creating an equivalent RNA copy of a sequence of DNA.

translation The first stage of protein biosynthesis, during which proteins are produced by decoding the mRNA produced in transcription.

transposons Sequences of DNA that can move around to different positions within the genome of a single cell in a process called transposition.

For More Information

Canadian Genetic Diseases Network
2150 Western Parkway, Suite 201
Vancouver, BC V6T 1V6
Canada
(604) 221-7300
Web site: http://www.cgdn.ca
The Canadian Genetic Disease Network is a group dedicated to advancing research about genetic diseases.

Cystic Fibrosis Foundation
6931 Arlington Road
Bethesda, MD 20814
(800) 344-4823
Web site: http://www.cff.org
A nonprofit donor-supported organization that is working toward the development of the means to cure and control cystic fibrosis and to improve the quality of life for those with the disease.

Dolan DNA Learning Center
1 Bungtown Road
Cold Spring Harbor, NY 11724
(516) 367-5170
Web site: http://www.dnalc.org
The Dolan DNA Learning Center is an education facility dedicated to teaching students about DNA and related topics.

ELSI
National Human Genome Research Institute
National Institutes of Health

5635 Fishers Lane
Suite 4076, MSC 9305
Bethesda, MD 20892-9305
(301) 402-4997
Web site: http://www.genome.gov/10001618
ELSI researches for the National Human Genome Research Institute the
ethical, legal, and social implications of human genome research.

Genome Canada
150 Metcalfe Street, Suite 2100
Ottawa, ON K2P 1P1
Canada
(613) 751-4460
Web site: http://www.genomecanada.ca
Genome Canada is an organization dedicated to funding and managing
genetic research projects.

National Cancer Institute
NCI Public Inquiries Office
6116 Executive Boulevard, Room 3036A
Bethesda, MD 20892-8322
(800) 422-6237
Web site: http://www.cancer.gov
The National Cancer Institute is an institute dedicated to cancer research
and education.

National Human Genome Research Institute
National Institutes of Health
Building 31, Room 4B09
31 Center Drive, MSC 2152
9000 Rockville Pike
Bethesda, MD 20892-2152

(301) 402-0911
Web site: http://www.genome.gov
One of the National Institutes of Health, the National Human Genome
Research Institute facilitated the Human Genome Project and continues
to support and conduct genome research.

National Institutes of Health
9000 Rockville Pike
Bethesda, MD 20892
(301) 496-4000
Web site: http://www.nih.gov
The National Institutes of Health is the primary federal agency conducting
and supporting health research.

Web Sites

Due to the changing nature of Internet links, Rosen Publishing has developed an online list of Web sites related to the subject of this book. This site is updated regularly. Please use this link to access the list:

http://www.rosenlinks.com/gen/geno

For Further Reading

Allman, Toney. *Diabetes* (Genes and Disease). New York, NY: Chelsea House, 2009.

Barnes, Barry, and John Dupré. *Genomes and What to Make of Them*. Chicago, IL: University of Chicago Press, 2008.

Crichton, Michael. *Next*. New York, NY: HarperCollins, 2006.

Evans-Martin, F. Fay. *Down Syndrome* (Genes and Disease). New York, NY: Chelsea House, 2009.

Freedman, Jeri. *Tay-Sachs Disease* (Genes and Disease). New York, NY: Chelsea House, 2009.

Gibson, Greg. *It Takes a Genome: How a Clash Between Our Genes and Modern Life Is Making Us Sick*. Upper Saddle River, NJ: FT Press, 2009.

Giddings, Sharon. *Cystic Fibrosis* (Genes and Disease). New York, NY: Chelsea House, 2009.

Glimm, Adele. *Gene Hunter: The Story of Neuropsychologist Nancy Wexler* (Women's Adventures in Science). Washington, DC: Joseph Henry Press, 2006.

Gorp, Lynn Van. *Genetics*. Mankato, MN: Capstone, 2008.

Jones, Phill. *Sickle Cell Disease* (Genes and Disease). New York, NY: Chelsea House, 2009.

Kepron, Wayne. *Cystic Fibrosis: Everything You Need to Know*. Tonawanda, NY: Firefly Books, 2004.

Knowles, Johanna. *Huntington's Disease* (Genetic Diseases and Disorders). New York, NY: Rosen, 2006.

Lawrence, David. *Huntington's Disease* (Genes and Disease). New York, NY: Chelsea House, 2009.

Meshbesher, Wendy, and Eve Hartman. *The Role of Genes* (Sci-Hi Life Science). Chicago, IL: Raintree, 2008.

Panno, Joseph. *Gene Therapy: Treating Disease and Repairing Genes* (New Biology). New York, NY: Facts On File, 2004.

Panno, Joseph. *Genome Research* (New Biology). New York, NY: Facts On File, 2009.

Ridley, Matt. *Genome: The Autobiography of a Species in 23 Chapters.* New York, NY: HarperCollins, 2006.

Sawyer, Robert. *Hominids.* New York, NY: Tor, 2003.

Shreeve, James. *The Genome War: How Craig Venter Tried to Capture the Code of Life and Save the World.* New York, NY: Ballantine, 2005.

Shubin, Neil. *Your Inner Fish: A Journey into the 3.5 Billion-Year History of the Human Body.* London, UK: Vintage, 2009.

Simpson, Kathleen. *Genetics: From DNA to Designer Dogs.* Des Moines, IA: National Geographic, 2008.

Smith, Terry L. *Asthma* (Genes and Disease). New York, NY: Chelsea House, 2009.

Walker, Richard. *Genes & DNA* (Kingfisher Knowledge). New York, NY: Kingfisher, 2007.

Watson, James D., and Andrew Berry. *DNA: The Secret of Life.* New York, NY: Knopf, 2004.

Werlin, Nancy. *Double Helix.* New York, NY: Puffin, 2005.

Wood, June Rae. *The Man Who Loved Clowns.* New York, NY: Penguin, 2005.

Bibliography

Berger, Kathleen Stassen. *The Developing Person Through Childhood.* 4th ed. New York, NY: Macmillan, 1996.

Berry, Drew. *Molecular Visualizations of DNA.* Video. The Walter and Eliza Hall Institute of Medical Research. Retrieved September 1, 2009 (http://www.youtube.com/watch?v=4PKjF7OumYo).

Bio.com. "Dr. Craig Venter and Dr. Francis Collins Biography." Retrieved August 11, 2009 (http://www.biography.com/articles/ Dr.-Craig-Venter-and-Dr.-Francis-Collins-9542371).

Calfee, John. "Decoding the Use of Gene Patents." *The American: The Journal of the American Enterprise Institute*, May 15, 2009. Retrieved August 18, 2009 (http://www.american.com/ archive/2009/may 2009/decoding the use-of-gene-patents).

Cincinnati's Children's Hospital Medical Center. "Scientists Find Gene That Modifies Severity of Cystic Fibrosis Lung Disease." February 25, 2009. Retrieved August 20, 2009 (http://esciencenews.com/ articles/2009/02/25/scientists.find.gene.modifies.severity.cystic. fibrosis.lung.disease).

Dennis, Carina, and Richard Gallagher, eds. *The Human Genome.* New York, NY: Nature Publishing Group, 2001.

National Down Syndrome Society. "Fact Sheet." Retrieved August 11, 2009 (http://www.ndss.org/index.php?option=com_content& view=category&id=35&Itemid=57).

National Human Genome Research Institute. "ELSI Research Program." Retrieved August 18, 2009 (http://www.genome. gov/10001618).

National Human Genome Research Institute. "Timeline." Retrieved August 18, 2009 (http://www.genome.gov/10506099).

Nova. "The Cloning Process." PBS.org. Retrieved August 18, 2009. (http://www.pbs.org/wgbh/nova/sciencenow/3209/04-clon-nf.html).

Nova. *Cracking the Code of Life*. Video. 2001. WGBH Educational
    Foundation and Clear Blue Sky Productions.

Oak Ridge National Laboratory. "Human Genome Project
    Information: Gene Testing." Retrieved August 18, 2009 (http://
    www.ornl.gov/sci/techresources/Human_Genome/medicine/
    genetest.shtml).

Powell, Devin. "The 15-Minute Genome 2009 Industrial Physics Forum
    Features Faster, Cheaper Genome Sequencing." American Institute of
    Physics. Retrieved August 18 (http://www.eurekalert.org/pub_
    releases/2009-07/aiop-tfg072709.php).

Rabin, Roni. "Screen All Pregnancies for Down Syndrome, Doctors Say."
    New York Times, January 9, 2007. Retrieved August 18, 2009
    (http://www.nytimes.com/2007/01/09/health/09preg.html).

Sanders, Robert. "'Evolved' Virus May Improve Gene Therapy for
    Cystic Fibrosis." February 17, 2009. Retrieved August 8, 2009
    (http://berkeley.edu/news/media/releases/2009/02/
    17_schaffer.shtml).

Schwartz, John. "Cancer Patients Challenge the Patenting of a Gene."
    New York Times, May 13, 2009. Retrieved August 18, 2009
    (http://www.nytimes.com/2009/05/13/health/13patent.html).

Shreeve, Jamie. "The Blueprint of Life." *U.S. News & World Report*,
    October 21, 2005. Retrieved August 12, 2009 (http://www.usnews.
    com/usnews/news/articles/051031/31genome.htm).

Stanford University Medical Center. "'Junk' DNA Now Looks Like Powerful
    Regulator, Researcher Finds." April 23, 2007. Retrieved August 18,
    2009 (http://www.physorg.com/news96567418.html).

Sykes, Bryan. *The Seven Daughters of Eve*. New York, NY:
    Norton, 2001.

Than, Ker. "Neanderthals Didn't Mate with Modern Humans, Study Says."
    National Geographic News, August 12, 2008. Retrieved August 17,
    2009 (http://news.nationalgeographic.com/news/2008/08/
    080812-neandertal-dna.html).

Bibliography

Thompson, Dick, Frederic Golden, and Michael Lemonick. "The Race Is Over." *Time*, July 3, 2000. Retrieved August 8, 2009 (http://www.time.com/time/magazine/article/0,9171,997342,00.html).

Wells, Spencer. *Deep Ancestry: Inside the Genographic Project.* Washington, DC: National Geographic, 2006.

Wexler, Nancy. "Genetic Information: Its Significance for Patients, Families, Health Professionals, Ethics, and Policy Development." Comments to the President's Bioethics Council, September 2009. Retrieved August 25, 2009 (http://www.bioethics.gov/background/wexlerpaper.html).

Wingerson, Lois. *Unnatural Selection: The Promise and the Power of Human Gene Research.* New York, NY: Bantam, 1998.

Zimmer, Carl. *Smithsonian Intimate Guide to Human Origins.* New York, NY: HarperCollins, 2005.

Index

About the Author

Bridget Heos has written about health topics ranging from stem cell research to childhood obesity. She is the author of several nonfiction books for young adults. She loves researching scientific subjects, but this was by far the most interesting topic she has ever studied. Heos lives in Kansas City with her husband and three sons.

Photo Credits

Cover (top) © www.istockphoto.com/dra_schwartz; cover (bottom), back cover, and interior © www.istockphoto.com/Gregory Spencer; p. 5 © J. Cavallini/Custom Medical Stock Photo; p. 8 National Institute of General Medical Sciences; pp. 10–11, 43 © SPL/Photo Researchers, Inc.; pp. 12, 20–21, 54–55, 62 © AP Images; pp. 16–17 Darryl Leja/NHGRI; pp. 18–19 © Biophoto Associates/Photo Researchers, Inc.; p. 25 © BSIP/Photo Researchers, Inc.; p. 27 Shutterstock.com; pp. 28–29 © SIU Biomed Comm/Custom Medical Stock Photo; p. 32 Image Source/Getty Images; p. 35 © www.istockphoto.com/Matej Michelizza; pp. 38–39 © M.I. Walker/Photo Researchers, Inc.; pp. 40–41 Alex Livesey/Getty Images; p. 47 Cburnett/Wikipedia; pp. 50–51 © Univ. of MI/Peter Arnold Inc.; p. 56 Acey Harper/Time & Life Pictures/Getty Images; p. 58 Justin Sullivan/Getty Images; pp. 64–65 © www.istockphoto.com/Khuong Hoang.

Designer: Nicole Russo; Editor: Bethany Bryan;
Photo Researcher: Amy Feinberg